Teddy's Birthday

Copyright © QED Publishing 2004

First published in the UK in 2004 by
QED Publishing
A division of Quarto Publishing plc
The Fitzpatrick Building
188–194 York Way, London N7 9QP

A Catalogue record for this book is available from the British Library.

ISBN 1 84538 005 3

Written by Anne Faundez
Designed by Alix Wood
Editor Hannah Ray
Illustrated by Karen Sapp

Series Consultant Anne Faundez
Creative Director Louise Morley
Editorial Manager Jean Coppendale

Printed and bound in China

Teddy's Birthday

Anne Faundez

QED Publishing

The toys are up early. What's happening today?
They bump and they bounce; they're ready to play.

4

Now they are gathered, it's time for some fun.
It's Teddy's birthday; today he is ONE!

"It's my BIRTHDAY!" cries Teddy,
"I hope everyone's ready!

It's party-time soon,
Let's decorate the room!"

Balloons all around, flowers everywhere,
A banner on the wall, streamers in the air.

"Oh, wow!" says Teddy.
"Party now! Are you ready?"

9

They share out the hats in blue, green and red.
Teddy takes TWO to put on his head!

"Let's play some games," say the Twin Yellow Bears.
So they play pass the parcel and musical chairs.

They clap to the music and make lots of noise,
Big Bear, Brown Bear — all of the toys.

Amanda the Panda and Jimmy Giraffe,
Together they dance and soon start to laugh.

Fluffy the Bunny has made lots of treats,
Biscuits and buns, ice-cream and sweets.

Everyone's hungry. They each find a seat.
With tummies a-rumbling, they tuck in and eat.

Next, there's a cake on a big silver dish.
Teddy blows hard and then makes a wish.

The toys clap their hands and together start singing.
Teddy is happy and cannot stop grinning.

"Happy Birthday to you, Happy Birthday to you!
Happy Birthday, dear Teddy! Happy Birthday to you!"

There's a gift for Teddy.
He's very excited.
A new bouncy ball!
He's truly delighted!

The toys are now yawning. Such sleepy heads!
They put on pyjamas and climb into bed.

After such an exciting and busy, busy day,
They close their eyes
And fall asleep ...
straightaway.

What do you think?

How many hats did
Teddy put on his head?

What colour is
Teddy's new ball?

Who made the tasty treats for the toys to eat?

Who is Amanda the Panda dancing with?

Carers' and teachers' notes

- Look at the cover together and predict what the story is about.
- Look through the book with your child, focusing on the pictures. Talk about the characters and what they are doing, for example, are they dancing, laughing, sitting down, lying in bed?
- Read the book together and then ask your child to tell you what happens in the story.
- How many characters are there in the story? Look through the book and count them.
- Ask your child to identify in the pictures the character whose birthday party it is.
- Ask your child to point to Amanda the Panda, to Fluffy the Bunny, and so on.

- Ask your child to draw a picture of his/her favourite character.
- Together, make party hats using coloured paper, glue or sticky tape and scissors. Talk through each step as you make the hats.
- Talk about your child's own toys. Can he/she describe his/her favourite soft toy?
- Talk about an adventure that your child's toys might have.
- Talk about your child's experience of having a birthday. What was the best part of the day?
- Together, make up a new adventure for the characters in the story, in which, for example, they go to the park or have an outing to the seaside.